Protected For Purpose:

A Journey To Destiny
Part One

Written By: Katrina Chanel

Copyright© 2017 by Katrina Fordham

All rights reserved under International Copyright Law. Contents and/or cover may not be reproduced in whole or in part in any form without the express written consent of the publisher.

All Scriptures, unless indicated, are taken from the KING JAMES VERSION (KJV): KING JAMES VERSION, public domain.

Scriptures marked NKJV are taken from the NEW KING JAMES VERSI ON®. Copyright© 1982 by Thomas Nelson, Inc. Used by permission. All rights reserved.

Scriptures marked NIV are taken from the NEW INTERNATIONAL VERSION (NIV): Scripture taken from THE HOLY BIBLE, NEW INTERNATIONAL VERSION®. Copyright© 1973, 1978, 1984, 2011 by Biblica, Inc.™. Used by permission of Zondervan

Names have been changed to protect the identity of each character.

Publishing Coordination by Brown & Duncan Brand (BandDBrand.com)

ISBN: 978-0-9984756-9-1

Library of Congress Cataloging-in-Publication Data
     Fordham, Katrina
Protected For Purpose: A Journey To Destiny Part One

Printed in the United States of America

This book is dedicated to my angel, my blessing, my son, Charles Alphonso Jones IV, his heavenly sister Emmani Chanel Obi (RIH), the late Paulette McNeil aka Aunt Polly, and the late Sgt Albert Dono Ware
May your lights continue to shine!

Acknowledgements

I would be remiss if I did not begin this portion of my book by saying THANK YOU GOD!!! You have made ways out of what appeared to be the end for me since I was old enough to remember and I just want to say thank you! Without you, I would have never given birth to the promise I have been carrying these years. I am humbled by your everlasting love for me and I am amazed at how much you love me despite my flaws. I will forever be grateful for the trust you have given me and I do not take your presence in my life for granted. I want to thank Dr. Pamela Kelly for spending countless hours editing my book to ensure it was kingdom ready. I want to thank Natasha Brown for lending her expertise and for her obedience as I embarked on the publishing process. I also want to thank Prophetess Lynn Warren for carrying me, for covering me, and for warring on my family's behalf for the past 3 years. It has been a journey but we made it. I would also like to thank everyone that believed in me because your confidence in my ability to finish the race, pushed me into my destiny. It was painful but now I know that it wasn't about me but it was God's plan and purpose to get me where he wanted me to be. Finally, I want to sincerely thank everyone that whispered a prayer for my son and I over the past three years, offered an ear to listen, and a heart to receive me for who I am despite my flaws. It will never be forgotten.

With Gratitude,

Katrina Chanel

My Prayer For Purpose

Father God, it is always easy to seek self-gratification when we accomplish tasks that present the most difficulty in our lives; however, I know that without you I would be nothing. I would not be the woman that I am growing to be without your grace; without your mercy; and without your daily dose of favor on my life. I would not be alive today had it not been for your hand on my life, nor would I be able to touch the lives of your chosen people. Lord, you spoke to me and said that the testimony I carry within is a testimony that is sure to deliver many from the snares of the enemy. Father God, I am asking you to allow your word to accomplish what it was set out to do. I would not have a voice of triumph in my life had you not given me the confidence to share how you snatched me out of the enemies' hands. Lord, allow your will to be done and allow every reader to be led by your spirit, as they turn each page. Allow the words to flow in a prophetic way that will reach the hearts of those that yearn to know you deeper. Allow them not to see my story as it is told, through my eyes, but allow them to feel your presence as they digest each word. Lord, allow your light to shine in the sea of darkness that creates an overcast in the lives of your people, including mine. I cannot take the credit for the victories I have overcome, because the victory is not mine, but they all belong to you. For it is by your will, that I can present these tests turned testimonies into words. It is my prayer that the words I share will ignite hope in the hopeless and awaken a supernatural faith in those that may have lost their "faith in you" along the way. I know that I am not perfect, but Lord purge me of my wicked ways and thoughts, so I can be more like you. Lord help me to be transparent, honest, and let the truth prevail through each keystroke. Purify me Lord

Protected For *Purpose*: A Journey To Destiny

and be the strength that flows from my hands onto each key. Father God, allow this book to go forth and accomplish your will. Let the meditations of my heart and the words that may follow thereafter be acceptable in your sight, because I boldly confess that you are my Father, My Redeemer, and My Protector. In Jesus' name, I humbly pray. Amen!

Your Daughter- *Katrina Chanel*

KATRINA CHANEL

"Father, if you are willing, please take this cup from me.

Yet I want your will to be done. Not mine' NLT

(Luke 22:42)

Let the Journey Begin!

Table of Contents

Foreword 11

The Intro- All Aboard 13

Born A Star 19

The Ultimate Price 37

Unrefined Faith 53

Dreams Become Realities 67

Broken Pieces 79

A Heart Divided 89

Foreword

The smile that Katrina Fordham aka Katrina Chanel once wore to cover pain has been transformed. Today she walks in Victory sharing her testimony of how God has protected her. (Romans 12:2)… "but be ye transformed by the renewing of your mind, that ye may prove what it is that is good, and acceptable, and the perfect, will of God."

Katrina's testimony of hurts and attacks have left many in despair. However, Katrina's story is not one of despair; it is one of triumph. It is a story of the pursuit of purpose. Katrina knew approximately 15 years ago that she was destined to be here. She had a vision, specifically for this book, and has nursed it to fruition. Habakkuk 2:3 makes it known that although the vision may tarry it will surely come to pass. Katrina, I thank you for hearing from God, being persistent, holding on, and not giving up! Your blessings of triumphs are our blessing of encouragement.

Dr. Pamela Kelly

The Intro-All Aboard

Personal Journal Entry:

09/22/2011-"One innocent black man dies today. As the world seemingly comes to a screeching end, I am compelled to leave my mark on the world in print. "
Katrina Chanel

How many times have you looked back over your life and said to yourself "I can't believe I survived - that?" If you are like me, you have probably asked yourself that question more times than you can count. If you are like me, then the answer is always the same! "I really don't know!" Is that truly the answer?

Over the past 35 years of my life, I found myself in what seemed to be continual valley experiences. I was always wondering how and if I would make it through each season. Time after time, disappointment after disappointment, hurt after hurt, I found myself trying to cover my scars with the best makeup money couldn't buy... "a smile." The smile everyone else saw wasn't really a smile at all. It was an outward representation of what I wished for inside.

In the fall of 2011, while traveling in Arizona, God planted the vision of this book in my mind. The idea etched in my thoughts started with zeal one way. Over time it became just an idea, no action followed. The title changed several times and so did the purpose of the book. At first, I wanted it to be somewhat of an autobiography; however, I often said to myself "people don't even like me; who is going to actually sit down and read a book about me?" Seriously, how would an autobiography, about me, my life, and my trials really help people? In my conflicted mind, I did a bit of rationalizing. I was not a famous figure from history or a highly-acclaimed actress. Who would listen to me? In my eyes, I was just a southern girl born in Panama to a military family, reared on a little street across the river.

Eventually my questions were answered. Time went on (because we all know that it waits for no one), the days turned to weeks, the weeks turned to months, and the months turned into 35 years! Life's tests became more challenging. Spiritual attacks on my life became more vicious. Often, I found myself at the bottom of the valley with no one to call on, or so I thought; perplexed about ending up in the same dark places repeatedly!

Then it happened! One day I cried out to God- seeking answers! It sounds cliché, right? I know, but it's the truth! Even in His word (Matthew 7:7), it is stated, *"ask and ye shall receive, knock and the door shall be opened."* At that moment, I had no other choice but to ask the questions that I had been trying to avoid all of my life. Questions, I really didn't want the answers to at that time. I asked anyway, *"Lord what is Your Purpose for my life? Why am I here? Help me to understand Your Will for my life because I am lost."* I asked all these questions not realizing that I had already been given the answers. I was and had been taking an open book test, all along…..it was called life. Realization didn't emerge until long after the tests were over. For every tear that fell, for every earth-shattering heartache, and every time someone else walked away; I was being strengthened in ways unseen to me. I was in the fire being refined on my way to becoming pure gold. I was being chiselled away like a diamond under pressure. I then began to realize that I endured some of the darkest seasons of my life, simply, to be a light during someone else's storm. My story is an illustration of an overcomer with a desire to inspire others to overcome in spite of the many hardships they may face.

As time, has passed, my relationship with God continues to improve and strengthen. He has shown me that the road I have traveled wasn't solely for me. My life testimony wasn't a punishment despite what I thought; it has always been a privilege. I was being shaped on the potter's wheel for others to see that even the ugliest piece of clay can end up being a beautiful piece of art. To be shaped you must be pressed, molded, and sometimes completely destroyed before you actually become the masterpiece you were intended to be.

This book isn't for the person that has it all together. If that's you then you just wasted your money. This book isn't for the person that has never experienced struggle, disappointment, rejection, or abandonment. It surely isn't for the person that appears to have it altogether, but is silently dying inside. This book is one filled with purpose and triumphs that will hopefully inspire and motivate the hopeless. It is the journey of a little girl whose life has always been destined for purpose, despite the enemies' attempts to derail. This is MY story……the story of how I was protected for you….the story of how I was protected to be an outward representation of God's divine PURPOSE. So, get on board and travel with me because we have a mission to complete and it's called Destiny.

Personal Journal Entry:

09/22/2011 - I can see myself on the Monique Show now sitting on the couch talking about my book. In some ways, I feel that writing is my gift.

Katrina Chanel

Stop Number One
Born A Star

Protected For *Purpose*: A Journey To Destiny

Personal Journal Entry

October 10, 2007- "I wonder why the Lord favors me so much despite my negative ways. I guess he sees my intent and my heart. - Katrina Chanel

In the beautiful country of Panama, I was born on February 17, 1981 at four o'clock in the afternoon to a military father and a Savannah belle. The birth of a child is a joy that brings families together and typically reminds them of their purpose to love. My birth on that day would mark the beginning of a journey that would ultimately take me to a place so dark that death was the only light I could see. How did I get to that dark place? Where did I find light?

I can remember yelling and hearing my muffled screams, as I squirmed trying to free myself from the crochet blanket covering my face. The beautifully crocheted receiving blanket was knitted by my godmother. The welcoming gift now served a nearly fatal purpose, in the hands that once tenderly wrapped me in the same blanket. My mother Paula Jeanne, under the control, or out of control should I say, thanks to one of her many drunken rages was trying to kill me. There I lay, on the floor of our project apartment in Rose Hill screaming for help, as my mother (the woman I loved), viciously tried to suffocate me!

I couldn't understand why she wanted to kill me. I was only a child. I remember thinking, *"Would I have done so badly that she didn't want me to live anymore? Was it because I used more water than the once a week bath that my brother and I were entitled to? Was it because I smelled bad?"* As a child, I had no idea what could make my mother be so cruel to me. In my eyes, she was my hero and one of the most beautiful women in the world. Her long mink coats were flawless, her nails were always polished to perfection, and her Indian skin looked glove smooth, perfect! She was pampered by the men that always seemed to be readily available to help her wipe away the white dust from around her nose. Yes, the young inquisitive girl, me, had watched my mother from a distance in the kitchen with her many male friends, I thought her life was the life! I survived the crotched blanket incident only to later almost do my own self in, imitating my hero.

Mom was always the life of the party. People were always inviting her places and she was always very well received, well at least until the alcohol took control. My brother Dave and I always tagged along and were excited to be amongst the crowd. At any rate, this day she was sniffing white powder in lines. As a small child, I was very intrigued. Mainly because I thought I knew exactly where she kept the white stuff.

I decided then that I wanted to try some of the white powder too. After mom left, I opened the cabinet, grabbed a bag of flour and proceeded to dump a small amount out onto the dining room table. Following the sequences of activities I had witnessed, I figured out how to separate it into nice straight lines, using a piece of folded paper. I had no idea where mom kept the little silver thing she used for the lines so I had to improvise because I wanted the full effect!

Once I inspected the lines, I was then faced with the task of sniffing it up my nose. Now, how in the world would I accomplish this, then I had a "bright idea!" *"Right, I can use a straw!!!"* The straw worked! The minute I sniffed it, I began to cough and choke uncontrollably!!! The choking fit was so loud it summoned my older brother to my rescue. He promptly spanked my buttocks, after he made sure I was ok, of course. This wouldn't be the first time that my brother would save my life. Little did I know, it would be one of the many times God would spare my life too!

My mother wore the stench of alcohol like a well-crafted garment from an expensive store. It was her daily antidote. Alcohol soothed the pain she felt after my father finally walked away from the abusive relationship they called marriage. I can recall her being upset because he moved on and taking her anger out on us (my brother and I).

It was not unusual for me to be allowed my own ice cold drink in the cool, grey can with the blue bull on the front. The taste was bitter but to a five-year-old little girl I was, it was just a special kind of soda. As I grew older, I realized it wasn't a soda at all. It was actually beer! Parties, beer, music, and alcohol painted the picture of life for me. Men rubbing on women, women kissing on men, and drunk laughter billowing through the halls, all of these visions were a part of my fairytale life. The life where I got to pretend and act like I was a grown up too!

The fairytale I was living quickly became a nightmare the night I was awakened by my babysitter's nephew. I remember feeling the radiating pain between my legs as he molested me. I tried to cry out for help but his hand, which was covering my mouth, was too big for my small fingers to pry away. At that moment, my life changed forever. I tried to tell my mother but the drugs didn't allow her to hear me. She didn't want to hear what I had to say. My voice was trapped in a box like a mouse in a trap.

Interwoven and amidst the season of abuse and stifled voices, abuse and pain, the babysitter that was connected to the molestation I endured ironically was also connected to my first knowledge of God. One thing I can remember about Ms. Lucille is that she always talked about God and how much she loved Him. Now, I had no idea who

God was or why He was so important at the time. But I can recall her putting my brother and I on a big bus that took us to vacation bible school. This was the very first time I heard about God. We learned a lot in vacation bible school. We learned about a garden which I now know was the Garden of Eden and we learned about the creation of the world. The teacher taught us about the ark and the great flood that God used to destroy the world because of all of the sin that had overtaken it. I remember vividly, being afraid because I didn't want to be consumed by water for being bad. The remainder of my first encounter with God is a blur. I do however, remember hearing them sing songs and encouraging us to do the same. The closing ceremony for vacation bible school included a big play and we all had speeches that we had to recite. Looking back on it now, those plays were fun. We were also given certificates at the end. I couldn't wait to show my mom when she came back from her trip.

Sadly, Ms. Lucille also distorted my new view of God. The jolly plump woman was not so jolly when I told her about how her nephew assaulted me. The day following the attack, I tried to tell Ms. Lucille what her nephew had done; but when I did, she yelled at me! She almost made my small heart stop! She called me a liar and said that God didn't like liars. That's when I learned about hell because she told me that was where liars went. The more she yelled the smaller and smaller I felt. I was never quite sure what my mom understood about the event but we never stayed with Ms. Lucille again!

Summer ending and leaves falling, marked the beginning of a sequence of events that would ultimately leave my heart scarred forever. As a small child, I had no idea that all these occurrences would follow me, impact me, throughout the days of my life. The events that followed would create a foundation for my future.

It was a snowy day in my hometown of Fayetteville, NC. It was the first big snow the city had seen in quite a long time. My father and his new lady friend (who later became his wife) had already been to visit for the weekend. They were now on their way out of town to see his "lady friend's" sister. They asked us to tag along but mom always had a way of persuading us to decline. My brother and I, were excited to see all the snow on the ground. We played outside with all the other kids for hours, making snow angels, and throwing snowballs. As Dave and I played outside, we noticed the crowd began to thin out as each parent called for their children to come inside. As the sun began to set, we headed home too; only to find that our mother was not there – she was gone. The door was locked. Her car wasn't in her usual parking space. We were stuck out in the cold, we had nowhere to go. We hadn't eaten in hours; we were cold, and hungry. As we sat on the stairs trembling waiting for our mother to return, my brother pulled me closer. We huddled together to keep warm, no avail – we were chilled to the bone, until! A lady, with a friendly voice, stopped to ask my brother if our mom was at home.

She bundled us up and took us to her home which was two doors down. She gave us hot chocolate and offered us some food. As time passed, I noticed that the neighbor would periodically leave and come back. The last time she left and came back she said we could put on our coats because our mother was back. She then walked us down to our apartment where our mother greeted us with a small smile. I was not prepared for what happened next, the unthinkable. After our mom exchanged kind words with the neighbor, she sent us upstairs. I was sitting on her bed waiting for her, when I heard loud footsteps storming up the stairs. As she bent the corner of the room, I remember seeing something shiny in her hand. It was the butcher knife with the white handle from our kitchen. She pushed me down on the bed and began to scream superlatives at me that I couldn't even understand. She put the knife to my throat. I felt her press down, as it began to sting, I heard my brother call her name. I looked over to my right at him standing there with fear stricken eyes staring back at me. My mother asked him if she should let me live. He replied, "Yes," and with this cry of desperation she yanked me up! This would be the second time that my brother saved my life. Looking back on it now, I truly believe this is the moment where God began to put the pieces of the puzzle together to create the woman I was to become.

The days and months to follow would prove to be some of the hardest days of our lives. Plagued by violence, substance abuse, and several near-death experiences, my brother David would be permanently scarred physically. I would be scarred from invisible emotional wounds. The abuse ended the day my mother packed us up in her car and drove us downtown. As we pulled up, I noticed that it was the social services building that we often frequented. As a child we were taught that Social Services was the place that all the abandoned, abused, and neglected kids would go. It was always packed, but this day the parking lot was empty and nobody was there. My mother took us out of the car with our backpacks and told us to sit on the steps. She kissed us and we sat there as she drove away. Shortly thereafter, employees began to enter the building. A few of them walked past us while others stopped and looked. Eventually someone stopped and brought us inside. Not long after, like always our father's lady friend showed up to save the day. I would see my mother a few more times after that but we never stayed with her again full time. I recall visiting her on my 7th birthday; she was just lying there in a hospital bed. I had no idea that would be one of the last times I would see her for a really long time.

After my mother and father settled their divorce, my

mother relinquished her parental rights to my father and sailed off into the sunset. I wouldn't see her again until my 21st birthday. Much of my life's milestones occurred without her. I would never know the sacred love normally shared between a biological mother and her child. That void left me hopeless and afraid. It made me numb to the things of life and the thought of God was the least of my concerns.

My mother missed most of my greatest moments in life. She missed my high school graduation, she wasn't a part of my college acceptance process, she had no idea how smart her baby girl would become, she had no idea that I would excel in school or that I would compete in Spelling bees…. she had no idea that I would travel the world or be successful in the military…I would accomplish these things without her. As ironic as it may seem, although she wouldn't be responsible for leading me to Christ my interactions with her as a child would be the driving force that would eventually drive me straight into His arms.

After the divorce, my father, and my stepmother, whom I would later call momma Jay, gained custody of my brother and I. Bitter from the separation, it was very hard for me to accept Momma Jay into my life. But Momma Jay would be the one to teach (from 7 years old on) me the fundamentals a little girl needed to know. She would be the one to tell me what a menstrual cycle was and what it meant. She would be the one to teach me how to act like a lady and cross my legs. She was the one responsible for my transformation, post-divorce. She had her work cut out for her!

Prior to the divorce, before my dad kept us full time, I recall being isolated in my classroom, in a corner away from my classmates. My body odor (B.O.) reeked. So, the teacher sat me apart from the rest of the kids, since they had complained about my B.O. My hair was never combed (unless Momma Jay had it done); therefore, it wasn't clean. I sat at the back of the classroom until one day my father popped in to check on me.

These were the days when we stood up in class and said the pledge of allegiance before the start of each school day. Remember that? Surely you do. These were the days when prayer was still allowed in the schools. Man, those were the days. Smh. God was important to EVERYONE including school officials. Whatever happened to his presence? Hmph. I often wonder myself. Sometimes I wonder how different things might have been had God been my classmate every day? Interesting question!

Anyway, let's get back to the story. This day, my dad came to surprise me at school and noticed that I was in the corner and of course as a parent he asked, why? The teacher explained to him that the kids were complaining about his daughter's B.O. My daddy made sure that was the last time that they would talk about my B.O. Little did they know, I smelled bad because my mother never taught me how to bathe properly, therefore I did not know. Paula Jeanne never told me what my private parts were and she never showed me how to cleanse them. She was always too busy to care.

Sadly, Momma Jay would share custody of a 7-year-old little girl that did not know how to bathe. Momma Jay went to work immediately. Family friends donated clothes and shoes for me. Because I had nothing, I was so excited to have clean clothes and shoes. It was like Christmas for me every time Momma Jay pulled something new out of the bag for me to try on. We even went shoe shopping with her sister. It's funny now, but not so much then, Momma Jay's sister told her that my little feet were stinking. Upon further investigation, they discovered that the bottom of my feet were black as tar. This baffled Momma Jay because she knew that she had told me to take a bath the night before. What she did not know at the time however is that I wasn't taking a bath at all. I was sitting between the shower curtain and the liner playing with my dolls. Not because I didn't want to take a bath but I simply just didn't know how. I am surprised she did not smell me before then! It may seem sad but to me it was a way of life.

Later that evening when it was time to take a bath, Momma Jay told me to go in the bathroom like she normally would. She turned on the water for me and checked the temperature then she closed the door like normal so I started my normal routine. Playing with my dolls and letting the water run. Suddenly, the curtain flew back and there Momma Jay was standing in front of me. I was caught red-handed. At first, she began to yell at me for not taking a bath then she took a moment to pause then she asked me why I wasn't taking a bath. I was embarrassed and afraid, but I mustered up enough courage to tell her that my mother had never shown me how. Empathetically she took the time to show me how a little girl should properly cleanse her body. It was a moment that I will never forget.

Despite Mamma Jay's efforts, I always wondered where my biological mother was, although I would never admit it. In the back of my mind, I wondered if she would ever return. Much to my dismay, she never did. This "mom obsession" would ruin the relationship between Momma Jay and I for years to come. We disagreed so much that we didn't have the opportunity to bond the way I thought we should. This discord would also affect the relationship between her niece and I. This division would serve as a precursor to the fist fights and altercations that led to the bitter resentment we all shared towards each other. Instead of having a mother figure, I was left with a figure that resembled the shadow of someone that could have been the mother I never had.

On Dec 12, 2016, I visited that same social services building where my mother abandoned her two little children. I pulled into the parking lot, which has since been remodeled and I was amazed at the transformation of the building that once served as a reminder of my past. By this time my transformation was just as dramatic. Flashbacks began to crowd my mind but this time I was at the Social Services building for a completely different reason. I was one of the featured speakers on the agenda for an Empowerment Session. Isn't it amazing how God will allow things to come full circle? 30 years ago, I was left on the same steps that I boldly walked up that day, stronger than ever before, standing poised and confident. Yes, not merely a woman but a conqueror, an overcomer. For every tear that fell, God replaced it with pure joy, the moment I stepped up to the microphone to share bits of my story. This would be the beginning of my next chapter in life. The message from God on this day, "It wasn't personal, it was purposeful!" What a revelation!

Personal Journal Entry
October 10, 2007- I cried out to him and asked the hard questions. I got the answers I was looking for"-
Katrina Chanel

Stop Number Two

The Ultimate Price

Personal Journal Entry

July 17, 2006- Even though it seems like I had nothing God still left me with something, he left me with my will to go on.....

Katrina Chanel

There are many times in life that we often selectively forget things that we don't want to remember. Failed relationships, intentional choices that ended in turmoil, and hurtful circumstances that lead to a cyclic of pain. We have all experienced times when we wandered through life aimlessly looking for purpose; only to be frustrated when we reached what appeared to be a dead end! C'est la vie or such is life as they often say! All of the twists and turns of life can often leave you dizzy and delusional if you don't hold onto something to keep you grounded! For some, the delusional state is fueled by many things. For some it is alcohol. For others, it may be sex. For most…it is as simple as doing whatever it takes to avoid the reality that you are actually falling. For me it was a deadly combination of them all. Nobody wants to fail or fall, out of fear that they may be judged or shunned. So, people like me create this persona that only they believe. Not realizing that eventually you get tired of pretending to be someone else, besides the reflection you see in the mirror. This has been the story of my life until I decided to make a change for what seemed like the hundredth time.

Transition has been the signature brand of my image. Like a nomad, I struggled to take hold of a firm foundation year after year, month after month, and day after day. Why might you ask; because I never could seem to find my way back from the bottom? The key word in that sentence is "I". "I" couldn't find my way back, "I" couldn't let go of the past. "I" couldn't get over the disappointment of giving my all to others simply to be let down in the end. There is one obvious problem with that scenario. "I" wasn't supposed to be doing anything. Instead of trying to figure it out on my own, "I" should have trusted the God I was introduced to at the age of 5, but how?

How could I trust someone that I could not see? How could I talk to someone that I couldn't hear? How would I find the comfort I so desperately needed from an entity that I couldn't touch? These are my thoughts of struggle. How could someone that everyone praises and loves allow me to experience so much hurt and tragedy in my life, without doing anything about it? Where was God when I was being molested in my 5-year-old innocence? Where was God when my mother tried to kill me over and over again? Where was He!?!?!? I was angry. I felt alone. I was afraid. I was hopeless. I was LOST!!! I was in this place for years falling endlessly down a bottomless pit in the middle of a desert with no land in sight. My healing seemed like a mirage, unreachable/untouchable. The closer I got to it the farther away it seemed.

Can you imagine the hurt and desperation I felt??? I was pursuing a breakthrough only to hit the glass like a bird chasing its own reflection. It hurt! It is disheartening and it can be deadly. Deadly to your spirit, deadly to your soul, deadly to your mind, and if you are not careful it can be deadly to your body.

One of the most devastating times in my life that I can recall was the death of my daughter whom I will speak more about later. Her premature death is the turning point that led me back to Christ. It was during this time, that "I" realized that the God I couldn't see was omnipresent meaning he was EVERYWHERE (Psalm 139:7-10). It was during this time, that "I" realized that the God I couldn't hear was speaking to me all the time but "I" was always talking too loud to hear His voice. It was during this time, that "I" felt the touch of His hand on me as "I" felt the breath in my body leaving. Yes, it was during this time that God revealed to me by His spirit who He was in MY LIFE.

Journaling has been my life. I have always found peace in writing. As a young child, I often found myself writing as a means of escaping my reality. The reality is that my mother leaving me wounded me to a point that my heart was left bleeding. It was bleeding out into a river of endless tears that nobody could see but the pages I used to confide in. Writing was a means of coping with the pain that I didn't understand. I was a child. I couldn't explain the tingling feeling I felt deep down in my chest every time I thought about my mother and why she wasn't there. Now looking back, I realize that it was pain. Little did I know, that feeling would become a part of me for what seemed like an eternity; an eternity that would lead me to death's doorstep like a holiday visitor. The loss of my daughter accompanied by a myriad of several events that I will share later; introduced me to the concept of suicide or par suicide, since by the grace of God, I am still here!

Where did this journaling season of my life begin…..let me tell you. After a tumultuous eight years of bullying I managed to make it through my college prep years. For years, I was bullied by my peers. I was picked on and attacked often which placed me in a position to always defend myself. One incident in particular left me with bruised ribs and a huge knot on my head. My body was slammed in between the bleachers by the school bully as a result of a volleyball accident during gym. For whatever reason, I was never the popular girl in school and since my parents were strict most of the time, I didn't have a lot of the opportunities that many of the other kids had. Therefore, I felt justified to rebel. Like many teenagers my age, I was seeking acceptance in all the wrong ways. Fortunately, it never seemed to work for me. I have always been the odd ball out. Even now, I don't have a large group of friends but as I have matured I have learned that it's ok not being a part of the group as long as you love yourself. Loving yourself is the key to knowing your self-worth. Without that integral aspect, you are sure to be constantly searching for validation from others. I know this feeling all too well because I battle with it even to this day so don't feel alone if you have struggled with it too! I have always been the girl that nobody really wanted to be friends with because I wasn't a part of the cool crew. This "need" to be accepted, in addition to the bullying that I endured, led me down a path of worthlessness and low self-esteem that I fought to disguise.

I often acted out at home because I did not have the relationships that my peers seemed to have. I always felt that they had it better than I did when I had no idea how they were living or what they may have been going through behind closed doors. The lack of relationship and distance between Momma Jay & I worsened as the years progressed. This division led me into a state of sadness that words themselves could not explain. Momma Jay was very close to her sister's daughter and they always did things together like a mother and daughter should. They would often go shopping together, they would laugh together, cook together, and the bond they shared was one that I always wished I could have shared with my own mother.

Over time the jealousy and envy began to consume me. I lacked attention and I felt like I wasn't a part of the family. Even my father seemed to favor her over me at times and that made matters even worse for me. However, the only thing that they could see was a young teenage girl acting out. I wasn't acting out because I wanted to be bad, I was acting out because I lacked attention. My father, who always prided himself in being a man of very few accolades, was a hard worker. He was the sole provider for our family therefore he was not home very often. As my daddy, I often looked to him for the bond that I was missing from my mother and Momma Jay. But as a young teenager, I had no idea how to express this to him so I began "attention seeking" in other ways: running away from home, moving in with friends, sneaking and having boyfriends; anything just to feel like I mattered.

I often locked myself in my room and pretended to be someone else that was happy, simply because my outside environment was so sad. I began journaling, only to be placed on punishment after my parents discovered the things I was writing about them, especially Momma Jay. It never seemed to get better. We disagreed so much that we didn't have the opportunity to bond the way I thought we should. This would be the beginning of a long-standing history of emotional turmoil for me. I had plenty to write. This turmoil would lead to spiritual attacks that I could not understand. Dark shadows in the night and sleepless nights held me captive.

Momma Jay's sister was a very spiritual woman. We always went to church together as a family when "Mother," as they affectionately called her, was alive. I looked forward to these special moments because it gave me a sense of belonging. I enjoyed watching all of them primp and get dressed on Sunday mornings before church service. I was so amazed and smitten by how beautiful they all were. I wanted to be just like them when I grew up. They wore perfume that smelled like petals and the closeness they shared was a delicacy that I wanted to taste - family. I wanted to have a family of my own.

In 1999, I left for college as a means of escape, determined to have the family that I left behind. I received a full scholarship to college and the happiness I felt at freshman orientation can't even be put into words. I was finally on my own!! Free to be me, free to create a new identity, and free to be happy. I could not have been more mistaken. My early college years proved to be two of the toughest years of my life. I struggled to form bonds with the other students and the bullying seemed to follow me. My parents were now a distant memory because just as much as I wanted to leave, they wanted me gone. Although the distance was minimum, after they dropped me off that beautiful fall day, I wouldn't see them again for several weeks. Left to figure out life on my own, I struggled to fit in.

Despite my unpopularity, I secured the title of Miss New Residence Hall in the Fall of 1999. I was elated. It was the first accomplishment that I can ever remember. For the first time in my life! I attended coronation which was like the senior prom that I never attended. I was in the homecoming parade and once again, I felt like somebody special for what would be one of many "first times" in my life. It was amazing. My parents didn't attend the festivities; however, my aunt Polly was there by my side the entire way. Aunt Polly took me to JCPenney and helped me choose my very first formal gown and shoes. She stood in the mirror along side of me, looked at me and she told me I looked beautiful. The warmth that consumed my body at that moment was a feeling that I would not experience again until I met the very first love of my life.

It was Jam's 21st birthday and we were celebrating at the infamous Fat Daddy's sports bar and grill. It was always lit because it was the hot spot in my hometown. It was packed this night and I was out with the girls. Amidst the noise of the celebration, I heard a deep voice say "excuse me" as he bumped my chair. I looked up with my drunken eyes into the face of this handsome chocolate brother with a Louisiana accent. It was love at first sight. The days to follow would be a whirlwind that I will always remember. We were together every day! He was in the military and he worked third shift but he always made time to come see before I went to class. I was in love!

One day during one of my class breaks, I received a call from a private number. I didn't recognize the voice on the other line; however, the lady told me that I needed to come down to the Systel building downtown. The Systel building was a staple in the area and there were several businesses housed within its walls. The lady told me where to go and what time to be there; however, she did not provide any additional specifics about the appointment. When I arrived, I took the elevator up to the 3rd floor and as the doors opened I was greeted by sexually transmitted diseases precaution signs. I was flabbergasted by the numerous advertisements about HIV, AIDS, Herpes, Syphilis, just to name a few. I knew that I had to be in the wrong place! Surely, none of this information applied to me! I walked to the counter and said to the receptionist "*I have got to be in the wrong place!*" She checked the appointment list and sure enough my name was on the roster. She asked me to have a seat.

A nurse soon came out to get me. She took me into

an office where a familiar face greeted me. One of the guys that I went to college with was sitting in the chair. The gentleman used to sing in the choir with one of my exes from college, so he knew me and appeared very sad to see my face. The information to follow would rock my 23-year-old world. Someone I had been sexually active with had been diagnosed with HIV and had given my name to the Center for Disease Control. For Real! I felt like I had received my death sentence. The next 14 days would be some of the most trying days of my life... I had to tell the new love of my life that I may have infected him with HIV. It was the hardest truth that I had to face. There was no family I could think to call, except my mother. See we reconnected when I was 21 years old and remained in touch.

During the 14 day wait, I found out that I was also carrying my first child. Yes, that heightened my stress level, HIV & pregnancy. It was too much! In the midst of it all, I mustered up the courage to pray. I had not been to church in years! I had no idea how to pray! I figured talking to God would at least mean something, even if I didn't have the perfect prayers to say. I prayed to God for mercy and asked him to spare my life. I promised him that I would never sleep with anybody else again if he saved my life. (Yeah Right but it sounded good) "Please Lord, have mercy on me. I am too young to die." On Day 13, I received a call from the same private number. This time, the voice was more chipper and her purpose for calling was more promising. "Your test was negative." God had heard my prayers. It was an example of his mercy and favor that I had never witnessed before. I was thankful and blessed to have another opportunity to make better choices.

Now what was I going to do about the baby? Shortly after God spared my life and protected me from the hands of death, my life changed again. My boyfriend (I mentioned I was "in love") came to me and gave me news that shattered my then existence. He had military orders to Korea for a year.

I was pregnant, facing homelessness, and I was lost! My grades had fallen in school, I wasn't focused, and in my mind, I still thought I had the opportunity of a lifetime. I had the opportunity to have the family I never had and marriage. Those dreams faded quickly when he asked me to have an abortion. Like many men his age, he just wasn't ready to be a father. Since he was leaving, he wouldn't be there to help me through the pregnancy. My parents weren't involved in my life consistently; my brother was gone; and I didn't really have much family to turn to now. What other options did I have? He wanted me to move to Louisiana to live with his mother and family but I didn't want to be a burden on them, so I declined. The decision was made to terminate the pregnancy. Once again, my "Family" dream was deferred and I felt hopeless. Thus the jubilation of the triumph of a negative test, slipped quickly into a valley of despair. But all believers know that a dream deferred is not a dream denied. It's just another opportunity for God to get the glory!

Personal Journal Entry

December 30, 2008- I remember being in this place not long ago and I messed it up putting my faith in man when I should have been believing in God. I am truly blessed in the midst of my storm"

Katrina Chanel

Stop Number Three
Unrefined Faith

Shortly after the termination of my unborn child, the love of my life took me home with him to Louisiana for one last visit before he departed for Korea. We had an awesome time together. His family always embraced me like I was one of their own and this visit was no different, one to remember. For the first time in a long time I was genuinely happy! We laughed; we feasted on Cajun-Creole delicacies, and simply enjoyed life. It was awesome! During our visit, the then love of my life, took me to the park. It was a warm day and the lake was beautiful. We held hands and walked by the water. We fed the ducks and watched out for the gators. Then it happened! He proposed. I was finally going to be a wife. It was unexpected and was a total surprise!

We planned to get married during his mid-tour on his break from Korea. For those of you that haven't ever been in the military, when you have a yearlong unaccompanied assignment they offer you the option to take leave at the 6 months mark to come home. I was finally on my way. I was hopeful again and things were finally looking up. I started going back to class and I was excited about my future. I had a reason to excel that was greater than me. One thing was missing, my relationship with God.

I wasn't seeking God nor was I spending the time with Him that I should. I wasn't even seeking His guidance nor His direction. I was figuring it all out on my own. I had no idea that I was doing more harm to myself than good. I was setting myself up for failure in the midst of trying to prepare for success. What I have learned over the years is that when you don't seek God in your decision-making, you leave room for the enemy to take control. And he has a way of creating illusions that take on the identity of whatever your heart desires. Like a chameleon, he (the enemy) changes his appearance to fit into the environment he enters and it can be deadly. The distractions can be so intense that you lose sight and miss things in front of you. It creates a fog, so thick in your mind; you can't think straight enough to understand what is happening around you. It consumes you like your favorite movie arrests your attention. The enemies ploy is to knock you off your path.

It's hard to recognize the enemy's tactics behind the disguises used; that are so well-crafted. As I patiently awaited my fiancé's return, I marvelled at the thought of being a wife. I was ready! At the time, I lived in the projects not far from the News and Observer with the bare minimum. My décor was simple, one folding chair that was from his barracks room that unfolded as a futon on the floor, a bookshelf, a TV he left with me, and a food tray that served as a TV stand. I didn't even own a kitchen table. My rent was only $25 a month and my light bill a little more than rent. In addition to school, I worked at a clothing company in the mall where I had been for a few months trying to work some extra hours. He also left me his car, so I didn't have to worry about reliable transportation. He paid the insurance and the car payment so all I had to do was get in and drive. Life was good! As it neared his return, the more excited I became. Much to my bewilderment he was changing. His conversations were becoming more and more vague. He was becoming distant and I couldn't understand why. We went from talking about getting married to not speaking about it at all which was very confusing to me considering we were still engaged. Then he came home.

The day he came home, it was obvious that his feelings were different. I wasn't greeted with the warm hug that he left me with. His demeanor was different, his conversation was different, even our intimacy felt different. There was a disconnection. But why? After his third day home, he broke the news to me that he was getting out of the military after his tour was over in Korea. I was confused. He then went on to tell me that he no longer wanted to get married and that he had decided to end our relationship. I was devastated!! The only explanation that he gave me was that he thought it was for the best and that he decided to go in a different direction with his life. He shared his future plans to move to Virginia with one of his platoon sergeants, until he could get back on his feet. Apparently the sergeant, "HE" was going to get him a good job there. I wasn't convinced.

He took his car, his support, his love, and when he left he took his promises with him. I was stranded, alone, hurt, and depressed. My life began to take a turn for the worst, AGAIN. I stopped going to class and I lost my drive to succeed. I had no idea what to do or where to go. What was I going to do now? I had nothing. I was making $5.25/hour at my mall job and I was only bringing home $60/month. How was I going to survive? I couldn't afford to pay rent, lights, and water on my own, without his support. I now had no car to drive and nowhere to drive to. Again, I decided to turn to God!

Why do we always wait until the bottom falls out to cry out for Him? We use Him as an option when God should ALWAYS be the priority. Yet He remains steadfast through it all and He always fulfils his promises to never to leave us (Deuteronomy 31:6), although we leave Him all of the time. It's amazing how wonderful He is and how much He continues to love us even when we turn our backs on Him. Amidst my dark depression, I started to spiral out of control. But, I cried out to God! I felt myself going crazy. I couldn't focus. I kept talking to God. All I could think about was what could have been. The only thing I could see was our future shattering like glass. I was trying to hold on to each piece but it cut me deeper the more I tried. I continued to pray. I wanted answers. I needed answers. And that's when it happened. I heard from God for the very first time and he answered my prayers. He revealed to me by His spirit in the middle of the night what was going on with the man. We are quick to seek God for answers knowing that we are not always ready for the truth but that never stops us from asking.

I found myself sitting in front of a computer screen reading an email from a young lady to my fiancé talking about the baby they were expecting. My heart began to break and with it the tears began to fall. I was in disbelief. Now it all was starting to make sense. He decided to end the relationship because he had been unfaithful and conceived a child because of his infidelity. The platoon sergeant that he was going to live with was the mother of his child. Imagine how I felt. I had aborted my baby to give him an opportunity to live life and six months later he was expecting a child with someone who he barely even knew. This was the beginning of my quest to find love yet again. I talked to any and everybody that would listen. This occurrence started the cycle that led to the loose lipped woman that I turned into over the years. The woman that most people would not be able to tolerate simply because they couldn't understand what I was going through.

I was the woman that could never keep her business to herself. I was the woman that was always seeking advice from others instead of confiding in the one person that could help, God! I would talk to strangers, I overwhelmed friends so much that they didn't even want to answer my calls most of the time, and forget trying to reach out to my family. What family? I barely talked to my parents during this time and I saw them even less. My biological mother lived in Florida at the time so seeing her wasn't an option either but we talked from time to time. The only support I had was my oldest brother, Flipper.

Flipper was my mother's son and even though he was only my half-brother, he treated me like we shared the same father. He drove cabs at the time and would often come by to check on me. He was a man of faith and he always had a word for me. He was always encouraging me to be more and not to let the circumstances of life consume me. I wish I had listened. All the pressure was too much to bear. I was working two jobs and still struggling to survive. One day after working a 15-hour day, I decided I would join the military. I went down to the recruiting station and visited each branch.

My dad was in the army and he always told me that he never wanted me to go there because it wasn't a place for women. He encouraged me to look at the Navy and the Air Force. He said those were the best branches for women because they took care of their own. According to him, accommodations during deployments were nice and they always had the best food. For once I took his advice. Shortly before I made the decision to join, while working at my part time job I met another guy that swept me off my feet. Cody was a nicely built guy that just happened to come into the store and he flirted with me a bit. His smile was amazing and he had the explosive personality to match. He was very cocky but confident which I found very attractive. As you can see the cycle continued, the need to be validated, the need to be loved always lead me straight into the enemy's hands.

Protected For *Purpose*: A Journey To Destiny

Still hurt from my failed engagement, I wasn't interested in dating anyone so we simply began to build a friendship. A friendship that was light and fun was what I needed to distract me from the pain. For the first time, in a long time I could laugh again. Cody came over often and I would cook for him sometimes. The first time he ever came to visit, we played a simple game called Mancala. The simplicity of it all is what intrigued me. He wasn't trying to sleep with me and he just wanted to get to know me; refreshing considering everything I had endured. I met a few other guys along the way but nobody ever took the place of my first love.

With nowhere else to go, an eviction notice on my table, and a suspension letter from school I was out of options. I decided to take the ASVAB. The ASVAB is the entrance exam into the military. I took the practice test and failed. So, I went to the bookstore and got the "ASVAB for dummies," book and studied for three days and sat for the exam again. This time I passed. I was off to the military but the question remained which branch? I had scored so high that my options were endless for jobs and branches. The first stop I made was to the Navy Recruiter. He talked to me for about an hour and right before he sealed the deal we had the conversation about basic training. At the age of about 11 or 12, I knew that I wanted to be a medical lab technologist. I had taken allied health science classes in High School and my major was Biology so I was in love with science. The mystery of science was fascinating to me. I knew I wanted to pursue the same field in the military. The recruiter found the job for me. I was ready! Well at least until he told me the details. As a medical corpsman, I would be required to train in San Diego, California with the marines. Wrong answer!!! The Marines?!?? Were they crazy? They had to be. Then to top that, the recruiters, asked me if I knew how to swim, which I didn't? "No." Then he proceeded to tell me the process the Navy used to train their enlistees how to swim; I was out of there!! There was no way I was going to be pushed into 13-foot water and required to learn how to swim. Yes, they may have had Navy seals on deck to save you in case you started drowning, but that wasn't a chance I was willing to take.

I ended up with the Air Force recruiter housed right

next door. They had the same opportunities that the Navy offered minus the near-death stunt. LOL! So, I was good with that! I signed on the dotted line and within a month I was gone. I called my parents a few days before I was set to ship out and told them when I was leaving. The day of my departure, I watched the door and the parking lot waiting for them to come. My heart sank as the minutes ticked away. The other parents hugged their children goodbye. During the short walk to the Air Force van waiting to whisk me away to the MEPS station, I spotted my dad's truck. He and Momma Jay (in the passenger seat) pulled up. Our time was brief but I was happy they were there to see me off. As soon as that sliding door closed so did this chapter in my life. I was off to my next adventure.

What God had in store would take me down a path that would transform me into the woman that I never thought I was capable of being. This would be the season of my life where I learned what it really meant to have faith. What did faith really mean? I had no idea, but the travels that laid ahead would be the greatest teacher I could ever have.

Personal Journal Entry

February 17, 2009- (My 27th Birthday) The past few years of my life have been a whirlwind of ups and downs. I am not sure why I keep repeating this viscious cycle. I need to really take this time to love myself again.

Katrina Chanel

Stop Number Four

Dreams Become Realities

July 3rd 2003, was the beginning of my military journey. Broken from the memories of my past, I embarked on this journey, one of uncertainty, new opportunities, and greater responsibility. I was officially on my own. I boarded the plane heading to Texas with a renewed mind, hopeful spirit, and a fresh blow out; on my way to basic training. Thanking God for the opportunity to finally escape. My time in basic training proved to be a very refreshing time in my life. I was in the best shape of my life and I felt like I was finally accomplishing something for the first time in my life. I was making my own money and I was making my own way, without relying on others.

I kept in touch with my ex-fiancé's family during my time there and their support kept me going. His cousin Nana proved to be a great resource because she had already been down the military path I was currently traveling. Nana gave me a lot of guidance. She wrote me often and provided me with the words of encouragement that I needed to endure the rigorous military schedule. It was my hope that I would be able to form some long lasting bonds with my fellow airman, but relationships still seemed to evade me. I still didn't fit in and I often found myself left out of conversations which started to bother me. However, I was so used to it, it didn't bother me as much as it used to. As the basic training graduation date got closer, I was getting excited about the end. I called my parents to notify them of graduation date. When they said, they would be there, I could hardly contain my excitement. On the day of graduation, I scanned the crowd for their faces and waited patiently at the receiving station for them to arrive with the other parents. They never came. Sad and hurt yet again!

One of my fellow airmen invited me to tag along with his family, for graduation celebrating. Even though I was with them, it didn't replace the emptiness I felt from my parents not being there. Worried, I tried not to let my feelings show; until we arrived back at the dorms for mail call. My drill Sgt called my name for mail and handed me this big box. Mail call was always an exciting time because everyone waited to see what was received from back home. We all watched each other open packages to see what they would get and share joy! I begrudgingly opened my box only to find a photo album and card from my parents, apologizing that they were unable to be there for my graduation. No reason was given just simply an apology.

My excitement quickly turned to disappointment yet again. It seemed like every time I thought I was getting ahead in life and making progress something else would happen to take me three steps back and I was tired of it. During my transitions, I graduated two more times and my parents never came to any of them. In fact, I never had any support as I crossed each milestone with the exception of a couple of friends that I knew from college. However, that never stopped me from reaching out. I never stopped calling or making the 9 hour drives from Mississippi to visit my family back home. I was determined that one day my efforts would be reciprocated and that eventually they would finally pay off. In time, my prayers were answered. See God has a way of doing things in his time which never seems to align with our time but we can't ever simply just give up. You have to find the strength to keep going.

In the winter of 2003, tragedy rocked my world, changed my perspective on life, and gave me another glimpse of who He (God) was. It was the week before Christmas, and I was stationed in Wichita Falls, TX. I was nearing the end of my second portion of basic training as a medical laboratory technician. This phase of my training was more laid back than all the others because we were allowed to have cell phones during off-duty hours and we were given a little more freedom. My brother Flipper and I talked quite often. He was always my biggest supporter and I loved him more than words could express. It was the Tuesday before Christmas Exodus was scheduled to begin and we were chatting on the phone about all our Christmas Plans. For the first time in years, we were all going to be together for the holidays. He loved to cook so he was sharing with me his menu and what he was going to cook. I mean he had a spread. He was excited! Excited, about us getting together, about cooking and he was finally getting a divorce from his deranged wife, which happened to be twenty years older than him. He had just moved into his own place and he was no longer driving cabs, he was working on the road for ADT security systems. Flipper and I were discussing the family portraits we were going to take and my excitement was building with every word. My brother David was coming, my biological mom was coming, and we were finally going to ALL be together under one roof. We were going car shopping that coming Saturday, after I flew in. He planned to help me purchase my first car. It was going to be a great two week break for me. "Little sister" is what he affectionately called me with warm endearment. I looked forward to hearing *"Little Sister."* We exchanged warm wishes and ended our conversation with I love you, see you Saturday.

The following Thursday as I prepared to leave for class, I noticed that I had a call from my mother Paula. I had no idea why she was calling but since Flipper talked to her all the time I dialed him back to find out what was going on but I got his VM. It was around 8 am. I didn't think twice about it because he was normally busy during the mornings scheduling his appointments for the day. I left for class and carried on my regular routine. Later that day after class was over, I came back to my room to change for PT and noticed that my mother had called me three more times. In my mind I thought that she was just tripping again or maybe hadn't taken her medications for her mental disorders. I picked up the phone and called my brother again but this time his phone simply rang busy. I was confused and tried to call a second time. Busy again! I didn't have time to call back and I wasn't able to call my mother back so I just shrugged it off, placed my phone back in my dresser, left, and went to PT.

Once PT was over, I called my brother again because it was unusual for him not to return my calls, especially after seeing that I called a few times. Busy again! I finally decided to call my mother back. She answered the phone and asked, *"Hey darling what are you doing?"* I told her I had just gotten back in from PT and asked her what was wrong because her voice sounded shaky. She asked me, *"are you sitting down?"* At this point, I was getting frustrated so I asked, "Ma what's going on?" She quietly said *"sit down baby."* So, I did. She said, *"it's Flipper."* "What *about him,*" I asked? "I have been trying to call him for hours." She told me she knew and that he had been in a horrible accident.... "Flipper is dead." My heart fell and my screams radiated through the halls. My brother was gone and with him he took a piece of my heart. The next few days were horrific. I flew home to be with my older brother and my mom to plan his funeral. The reunion that was supposed to be joyous was now solemn.

All of the abuse that we endured at the hands of mother started to resurface, the day my college best friend, Talisa, went with me to pick up Paula Jeanne up from my aunt's house in Lumberton. During our ride back, my mother, Paula Jeanne, informed me that she was transporting Flipper's body back to Savannah in the next few days. I was livid. How could she make such a decision without consulting my brother and I whom had been by his side for all these years? How could she take him away from the only family and friends he ever knew? His church family was there; my father who raised him was there, not to mention my grandmother, who also kept him for a while growing up. The car erupted in dispute. Talisa tried to calm me down. The trip ended in her being dropped off at the Greyhound bus station downtown. I left mama Paula there! Talisa tried to talk me out of it but there was nothing she could say. A couple of days later, I received a call from the funeral home that was preparing my brother's body for burial. The mortician informed me that if I wanted to view his body that it was imperative that I came right away because my mother was transferring his body out the next day. I rushed down to the funeral home where I met my father and brothers. The mortician warned us that his body was not prepared as I heard faint sawing echoing in the background. I was curious to know where the sawing came from. Afterwards, I found out that they had to saw one of his legs that had been almost severed in the wreck. They asked if we still wanted to see, of course we said yes. As we walked into the frigid room, I could see my brother laying there. A white sheet covered his body up to his neck. I walked over to see him and noticed a large gash on top of his head and bruising around his left eye. Other than that, he still looked just as handsome as I remembered. There I said my final goodbyes.

I purchased my first car, and I drove 24 hours back to Texas alone. Scared the entire way that something would happen to me, I watched every car intently wondering if I was going to be killed in a car accident too. The trauma from seeing my brother in that state was a fresh reflection in my head and it kept flashing in front of my eyes. I prayed and talked to God the whole ride back. I had so many unanswered questions. Why did He take my brother? He was so kind. He was so nice and, like me, he had a heart bigger than gold. The officer said that my brother had fallen asleep at the wheel and veered into the path of a sixteen-wheeler. I found that hard to believe, especially since he was such an energetic morning person. I didn't accept that answer so I prayed instead. I asked God to show me what happened to my brother. I wanted to know. I arrived in Texas late that night and I remember the old wise tale, *"if you think about someone right before you go to sleep, you will dream about them."* I prayed again before I went to sleep, hoping to see him. I had my first spiritual encounter with God that night.

As I lay sleeping, I began to see a bright light in my

dream. A figure began walking towards me and the closer it got I was able to recognize the silhouette as Flipper. His skin was radiant and he was smiling as big as ever. He was happy! I asked him if he was ok. He said *"yes."* So, I decided this was my chance to ask the question that I had been asking God. I asked Flipper, *"What happened?"* He responded, "I was looking down." I asked him if he was going to be ok and he told me yes. Then he added, *"you will be ok too. Little sis."* With those words, he disappeared. A few days later, I spoke to my brother Dave about his visit to the junkyard where they took Flipper's car. He had gone there to retrieve Flipper's belongings to include his cell phone. He mentioned to me that the phone was on the passenger side floor board and the time on the screen was the time of the accident! This conversation confirmed what Flipper told me in my dream. He wasn't sleeping at all, he had been looking down. To God be the glory for answered prayers! I prayed and He answered. God now had my attention in ways that He never had it before. I was ready for the next task.

Protected For *Purpose:* A Journey To Destiny

Personal Journal Entry

April 18, 2009- As hard as it may seem, I truly want to believe that I can move on. So many people have come and gone out of my life. I wanna live out my dreams. I wanna wake up one day and know I am fine."

Katrina Chanel

Stop Number Five
Broken Pieces

After the death of my brother, I was determined to make him proud. Joining the military was one of the main things he always bragged about. He was so proud of me. He had expressed an interest in attending my graduations; however, financial constraints prevented him from the ability to travel. I understood. My next duty station was Biloxi, MS. Keesler AFB was going to be new home for the next 13 months. The white beaches and casinos were the staples of this city, not far from the Crescent City of New Orleans. It was yet another fresh start for me. I was stationed here to complete my last rotation before being assigned to permanent duty station. It was a cool city. I finally started meeting people and making a few connections. My ex fiancé was still living with his daughter's mother and our communication was hit or miss. Sometimes we chatted but our conversations were very minimal because he always wanted to respect his daughter's mother even though they weren't together. I could somewhat understand, but I didn't like it! I had no choice but to respect it, so I did.

Airforce AIT was difficult. the course load was hard and very demanding but it was one of the most rewarding experiences that I can remember. I finally felt a sense of belonging to something and I was making progress. My credit was finally improving, I was able to save money, and I was on the right path but my loneliness still managed to consume me when nobody was around. I began to drink heavily. I drank everyday non-stop. I had the same routine. Every day, I would go to the cafeteria, get a grille chicken salad and a cup of lemonade to go. Then I would go to my room and spike the lemonade just to ease the pain.

I met one of my current best friends during my time in Biloxi. Farrah, as most knew her, was very goal oriented and driven. She was a great worker and proper. I was drawn to her personality and outgoing demeanour. She was fun, kind, and everybody seemed to love her. Naturally, I latched on to her like a leech. Like a little kid, I wanted to know everything that she knew and I wanted to be just like her. I still hadn't figured out that being "me" was the best option. When you try to be everyone else the world never gets to experience your added value. I had not grasped the concept that "me" was enough. I was still seeking and searching for answers. I still longed for validation from others. I sincerely wanted to change but I didn't know how. I prayed and asked God how I could change because I hated the person I was. I didn't like who I was becoming. It was a vicious cycle that I couldn't break.

During my on boarding orientation, I sat beside a little, pregnant, airmen named Denise. Denise was going through a divorce when I met her and was dealing with the type of hurt that I was all too familiar with. I could see the pain she was feeling but I didn't know her well enough to say anything. Over time, we began to bond and share some of our stories and we became each other's backbone. We became virtually inseparable. In fact, Denise is the only person that ever identified my drinking problem. See Denise knew about my past with my mother and she expressed her concern that I may be heading down the same path. So, she invited me to church. She told me that I needed to seek God and find my way back to Him. All of my life, God had been vying for my attention. He has given me so many glimpses of His power. He has shown me on countless occasions how much he loves me yet I keep running away. There is a popular gospel song with the following lyrics:

"You told me you loved me and I should make up my mind, you tell me come back now, but I keep wasting my time, Feeling so very weak, you say I can be strong, I feel I've gone too far you tell me to come home, you love me still.."

There God stood waiting for me with open arms yet the farther he reached the further away I ran. Reluctantly I took Denise up on her offer. I visited the church she was attending at the time and the seed that had been planted years before was watered and cultivated for growth. She saved my life and she didn't even know it.

As my tour, there continued, I made some friends, lost some friends and made some mistakes; however, I managed to maintain my sanity while still having a little fun. I became a master deceiver during these seasons in my life. I smiled all the time but inside I wanted to die! No matter what I did, I still had that hole in my heart that I couldn't seem to fill. Despite my church attendance, I was still an empty vessel. I didn't know at the time that it was a spirit that was holding me hostage. I wasn't knowledgeable enough about the things of God to know how to fight spirits. The spirit of depression, pity, pride, and entitlement were having their way in my life. I had no idea how to stop them. I struggled. I often found myself sitting in empty parking lots at churches, after hours, crying out to God to save me from myself because I knew something was wrong. I was broken beyond repair but nobody knew. My outward beauty always attracted men; however, my brokenness prevented me from having successful relationships. I was afraid to let go of my first love because in my mind I was never going to find another love like the love we shared.

I felt that way until the night I approached the security gate and locked eyes with Devon Capel. Man, Devon was tall, light skinned and had the prettiest hair I had ever seen. His waves made me sea sick they were so perfect. I was in heaven. Denise worked with him very closely and she played matchmaker. Devon was awesome. He was kind and coincidently he was from around the way, meaning he was from New Orleans. We often took drives there to just hang out. We spent a lot of time together. He was an avid football player and fanatic until he hurt his knee during a game. I recall him coming to visit me on crutches just so we could spend some time together. These were the subtle things that I often overlooked because I was so caught up in my ex. He was a poet and singer, and he would often write me poems and sing to me. I was entertained and flattered; however, I could never open my heart up to love him. That would later prove to be one of the biggest mistakes of my life because the love I was seeking he was more than capable of providing. He was knowledgeable about the ways of God and he was very smart. He was tough but fair and he always pulled out the very best in me. I grew to appreciate that as time progressed; conversely, I never told him. I wish now that I had. We talked about my ex and he told me that I deserved better and he never understood why I was so caught up in him. Honestly, neither did I. My ex-fiancé and I hadn't been together in two years at that point.

As time progressed, my ex and I began to talk more.

He told me that he had decided to move back home to Louisiana and that he wanted to give us another chance because he still loved me. Even though Devon had been my sounding board and companion, we weren't in a committed relationship so I there shouldn't have been a problem with me at least mulling it over, right? Wrong! I was wrong but I wouldn't realize that until nearly 10 years later. By then it would be too late. I accepted an assignment in Germany, I left Devon behind, my ex-fiancé and I married, and six months later he was gone.

Our nearly four-year courtship was over. Whoever said that the first year of marriage was the hardest never lied! Our marriage ended the night we locked eyes, mine tearful, his piercing, when he let me know, *"Have you ever had a leather coat? Have you ever tried on a new one only to realize that it didn't fit and that you liked the old one better! What do you do? You put the new one back right?"* I nodded, having no idea where this was going. He then followed it by saying *"well my ex is my old leather jacket and you are the new one. I have decided to go back to her. She is already broken in so it works better."* I was devastated yet again. This occurrence jump started the cycle of abuse that I thought I had escaped. But I had to live with reality that even though it hurt, I had also played my part.

Yet again I did not seek God's guidance before making a lifelong commitment. I did what Katrina wanted to do. There's that word "I" again. God was nowhere in sight until after the damage was already done. My lesson through it all....*seek ye first the Kindgom of God and his righteousness and these things shall be added unto you*" (Matthew 6:33). Surely after that you would think that I finally learned my lesson? Wrong again! He left me in Germany and with that I thought he took my sanity. I stopped eating and drove myself crazy trying to reconcile the marriage long after he was gone. Reality didn't hit me until I called his phone and realized that his old leather coat could talk. She answered the call and my world was shattered. I called and asked his girlfriend if I could speak to my husband. How much obvious did God have to make it for me to get the picture? Our marriage was over and my journey back to God began again.

Often God will take things from us in order to lead

us to something better. He (God) will allow you to lose some things so He (God) can restore them and nobody can get the glory except Him (God). These are some of the hardest lessons we as HIS (God) children must learn but they are necessary for growth. Like a seed in the ground, once you are planted, you get walked on, stepped on, and after being watered you eventually bloom. Then once you start blooming, it's time to cut back the blooms so the next ones can bloom bigger and brighter. God does us the same way and even though it's not easy, it is necessary. Like a garden, we must be cultivated so we can be used for his (God) glory and prepared for our purpose. Boy, was I pruned!!

Stop Number Six
A Heart Divided

My failed marriage became the catalyst for the pattern of abuse that soon followed. That situation combined with many others would serve as the platform that the enemy would use over the next 6 years to keep me bound. The cycle of abuse which was often ignited by lustful desires left me broken, abused, taken advantage of, and on several occasions, should have cost me my life. But God's divine hedge of protection covered me in ways that I never even realized. He was covering me long before I could even recognize it and he would continue to do so as the years progressed. Domestic violence wears many faces. It may come in the form of physical abuse which is the most common; however, the abuse can also be financial, emotional, or a deadly combination of all the above.

Painfully, I often wore each of them as a spiked undergarment covered with an invisible cloak disguised as happiness and a radiating smile. I exuded the appearance of a young lady that had it altogether. It's not easy covering up pain that seems to never go away. It's not easy looking at yourself and lying to others about what you are going through or in most case downplaying the severity of it. My spirit was crying out for the type of food that only God could provide. I have starved myself every day on and off for the past 35 years.

Suffering through failed friendships, relationships, and spiritual connection because of my inability to trust the will of God, because of my stupidity for refusing to walk away from the things that I knew weren't beneficial in my life. I have refused to walk away from the world and battled with myself, simply because I was afraid that I would lose the connections. Afraid that I would lose the connections that I had been so desperately seeking but in hindsight never really needed. The people in my life during this time wanted the best OF me not the best FOR me. My lesson through it all…Stop allowing myself to be so vested into others that I lose sight of what God created perfect in his own image. Others can only de-value you if you allow them to so mark yourself up!!! You are worth it!

I have yet to completely figure it out and I would be lying to you if I told you that the road to knowing and loving "me" happened overnight. It hasn't. It has proven to be a daily struggle, a struggle to overcome an addiction that medication can't treat. The addiction that causes you to crave the acceptance of others more than the love you give yourself. It takes daily affirmations from the woman I see in the mirror that I sometimes wish I could avoid. It can be hard embracing your value when you have been stripped of it most your life. It's hard to overcome being compared to an old leather coat when you have mink value. It's hard but possible! There are more valleys to discuss as we travel this journey but they all end in triumph!! These valley experiences and triumphs combined created the "ME!" I was destined to be. Before now, I never knew that I was a star waiting to shine! God had to reveal it to me through my pain. The example of victory that my life is becoming is a true testament of God's undying love for his children. And it is proof that if you simply let go of your desires and hold onto HIS (God) that things will turn around. Despite my flaws, God continues to protect me for his Purpose through it all! He (God) gets all the Glory for my life and as my story continues you will soon see how abiding in him through all things can do the same for you! Stay tuned for Part II, because it only gets better from here!!

Personal Journal Entry

July 17, 2006- "This time alone has shown me a lot about myself. Things like how strong I can be, and how I can still survive despite the odds. That even though it seems like I had nothing, God still left me with something. He left me with my will to go on..."

Katrina Chanel

About The Author

Katrina Chanel Fordham, CLS, is an author, budding motivational speaker and domestic violence advocate who currently works in the forensic toxicology field as a Laboratory Supervisor. Katrina's primary career goal is to offer support to individuals as they embark on their healing journey from addiction to freedom.

She is a US Air Force Veteran, with over 13 years of experience as a Clinical Laboratory technician. Katrina currently lives in Raleigh, NC with her beautiful son.

Visit her website www.iamkatrinachanel.com for upcoming events, future projects, and to schedule speaking engagements.

Cover Photos Courtesy of BrownBoy Photography and Graphics, Raleigh, NC

Hair by Phoebe Ward, JcPenney Salon, Fayetteville, NC

Lashes by LashNYu Master Stylist, Teonte Moreland-Thomas